The Seeds and Eggs of Life

Cree Cree

Archway Publishing books may be ordered through booksellers or by contacting:

Archway Publishing
1663 Liberty Drive
Bloomington, IN 47403
www.archwaypublishing.com
1 (888) 242-5904

ISBN: 978-1-4808-2894-0 (sc)
ISBN: 978-1-4808-2895-7 (e)

Print information available on the last page.

Archway Publishing rev. date: 4/6/2016

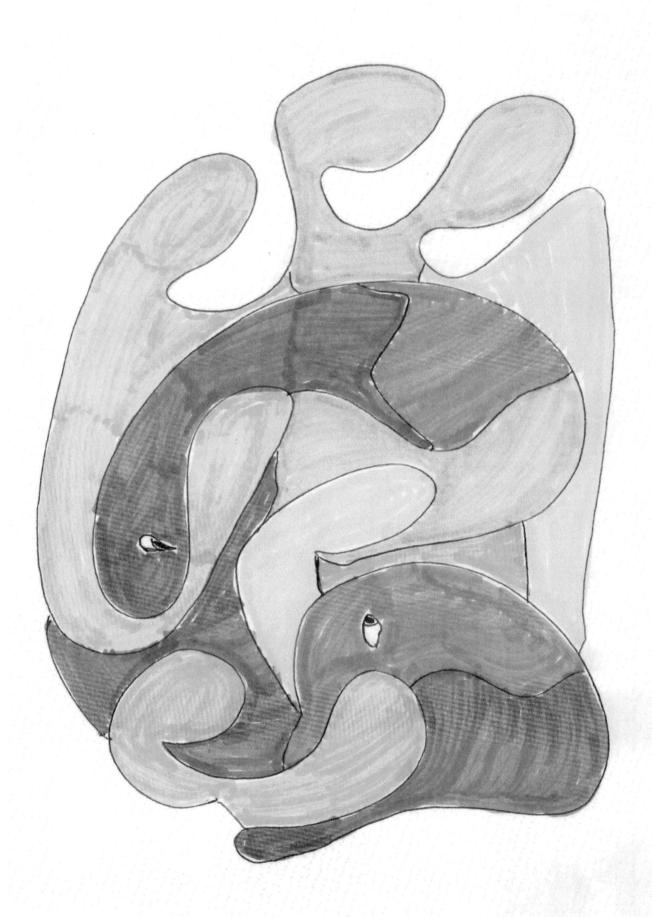

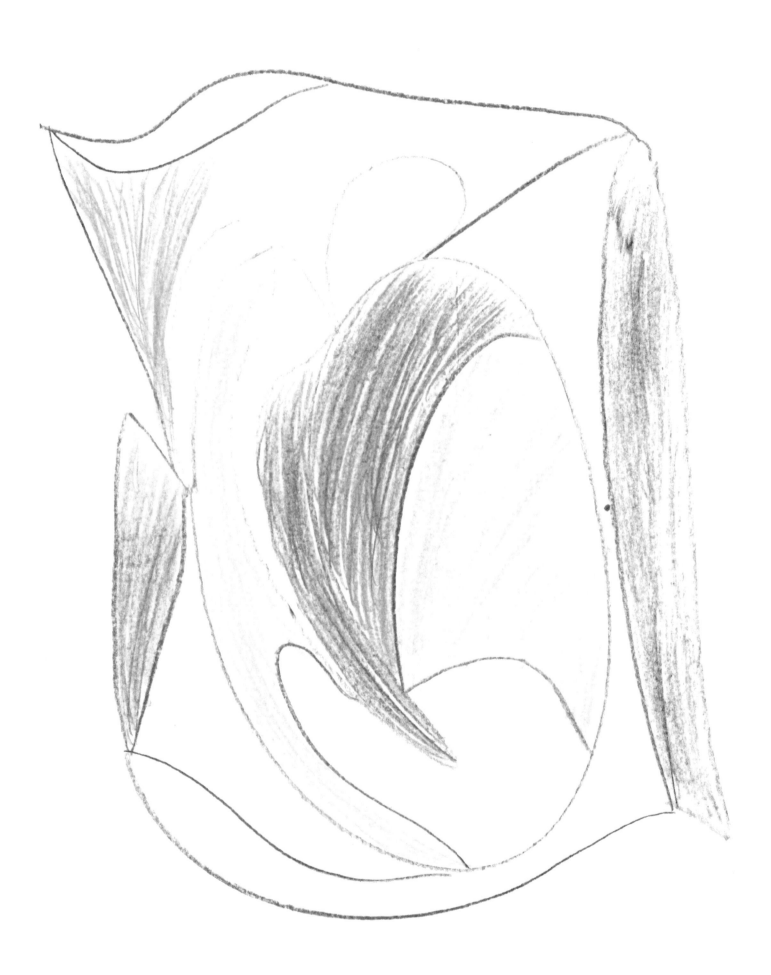

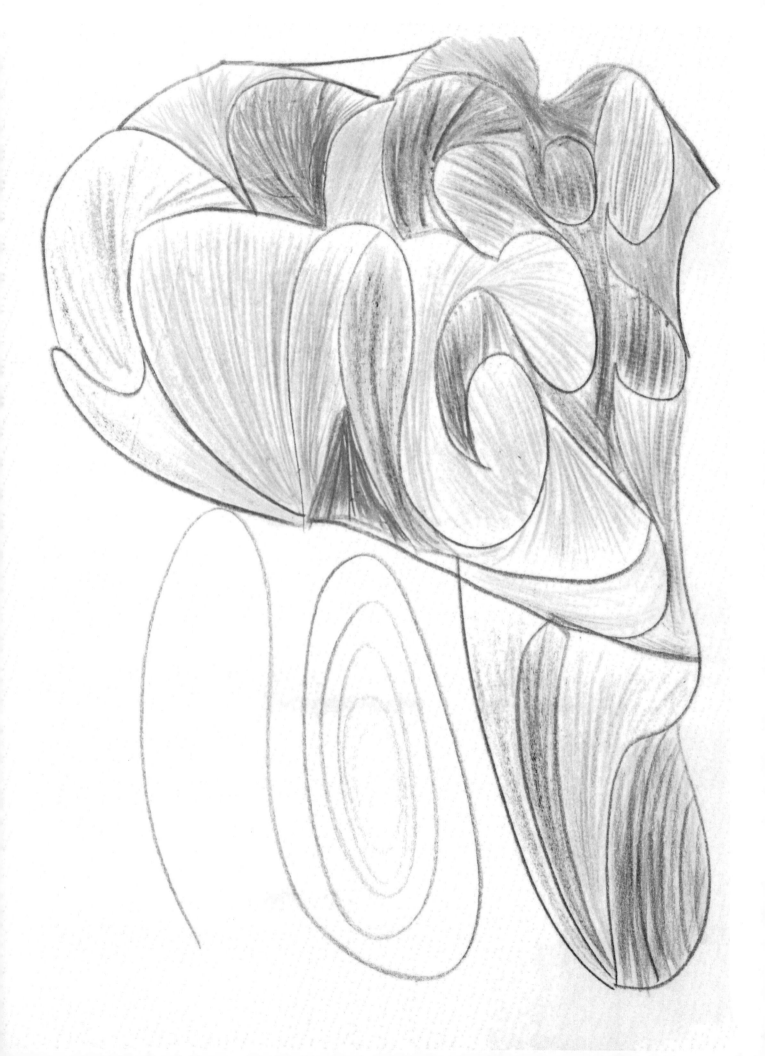

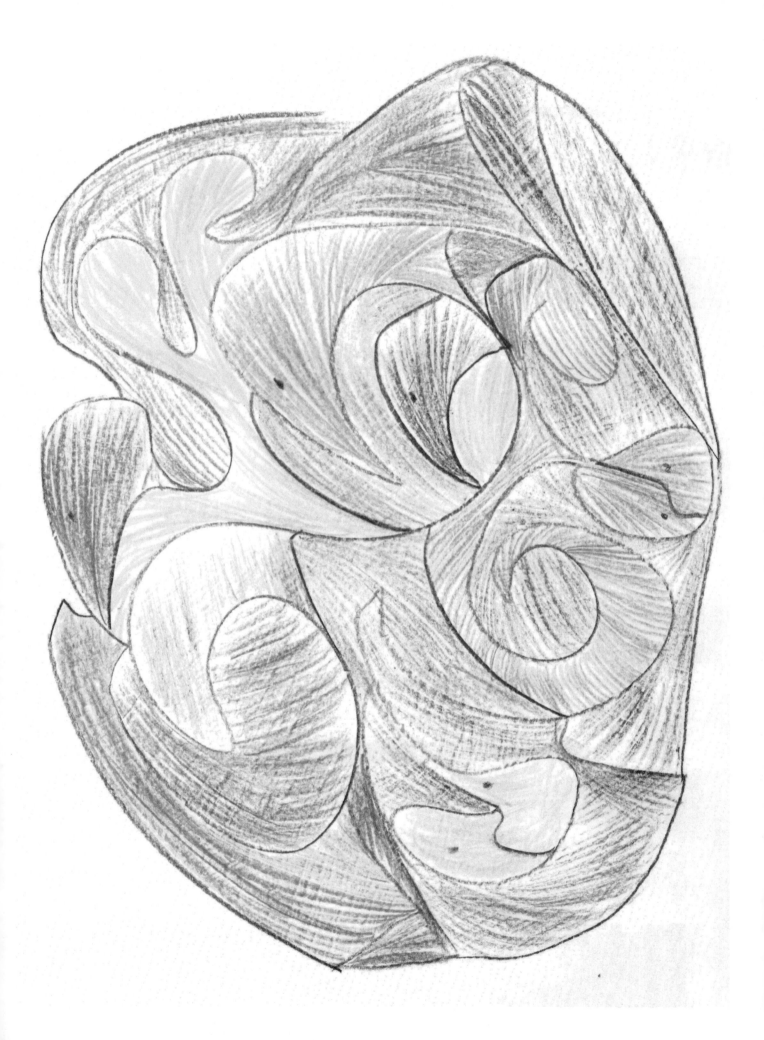

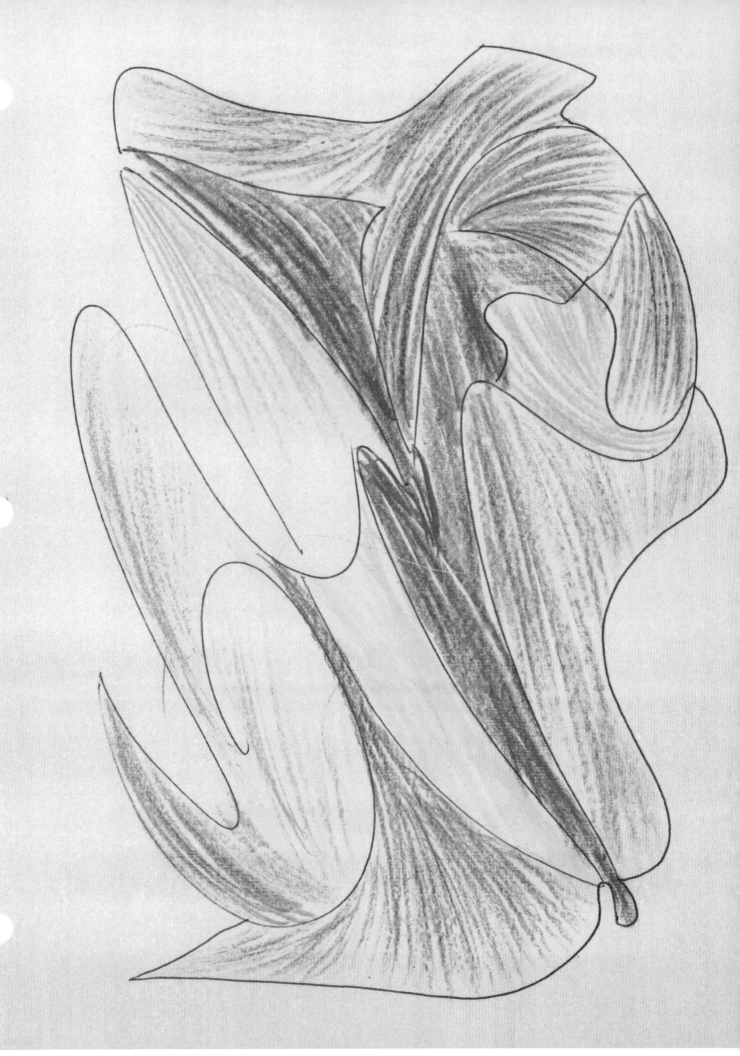

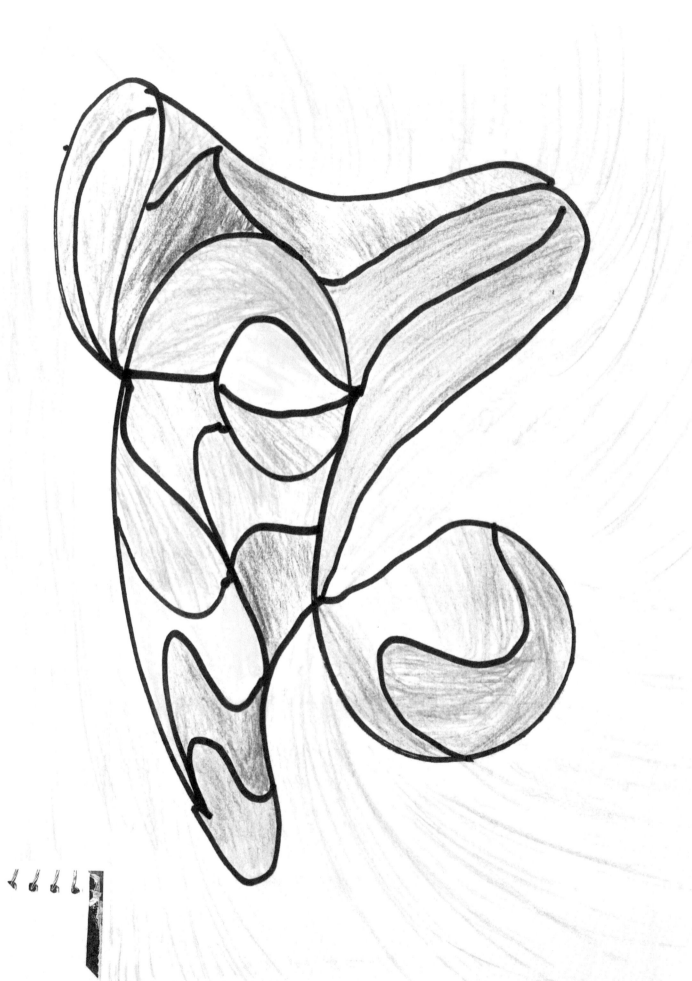

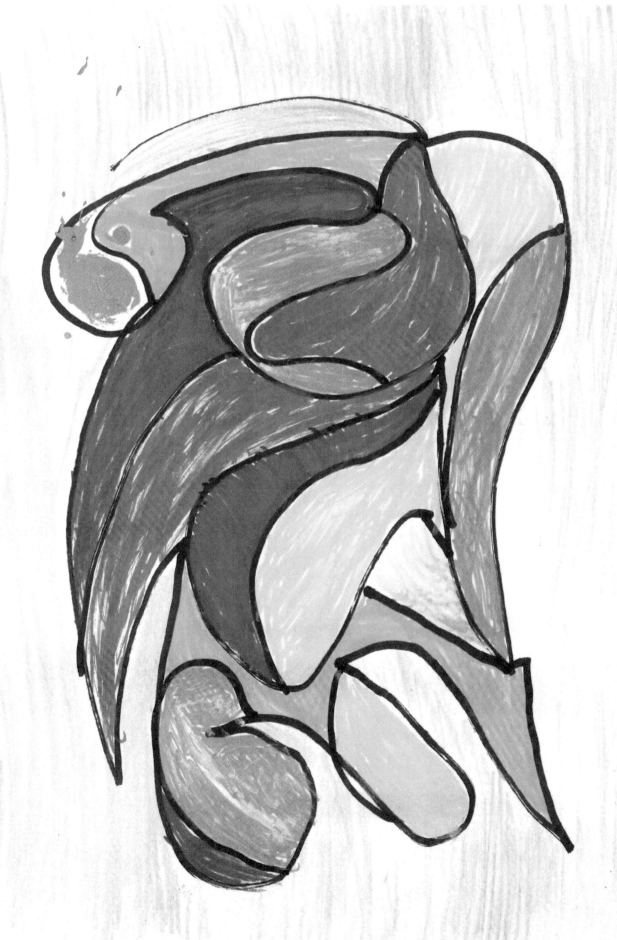

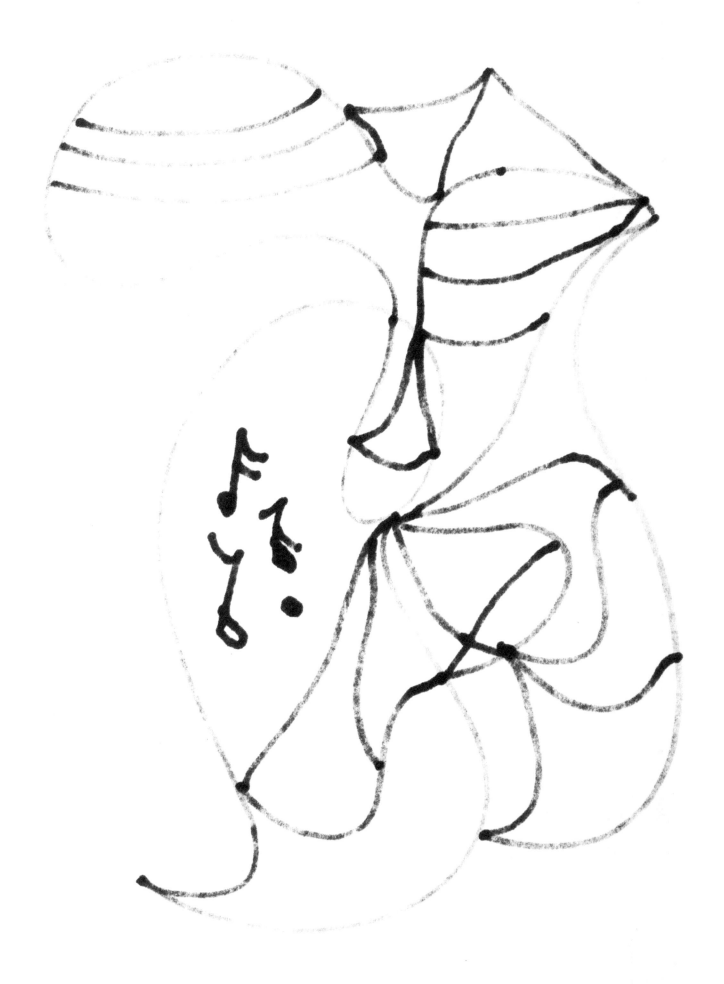

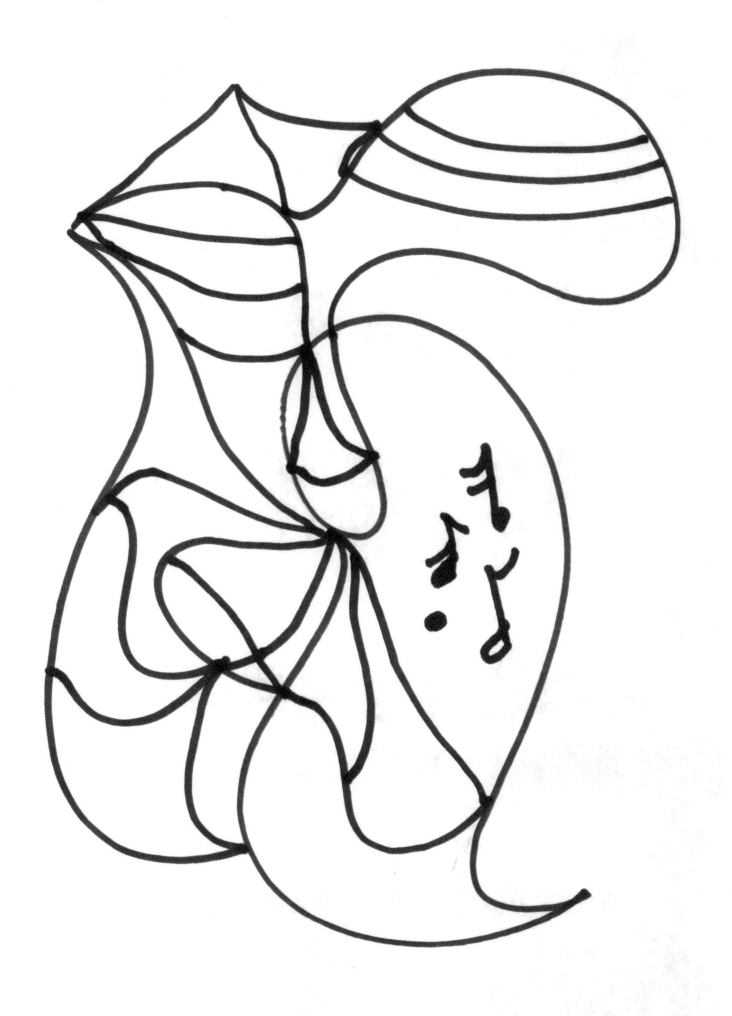

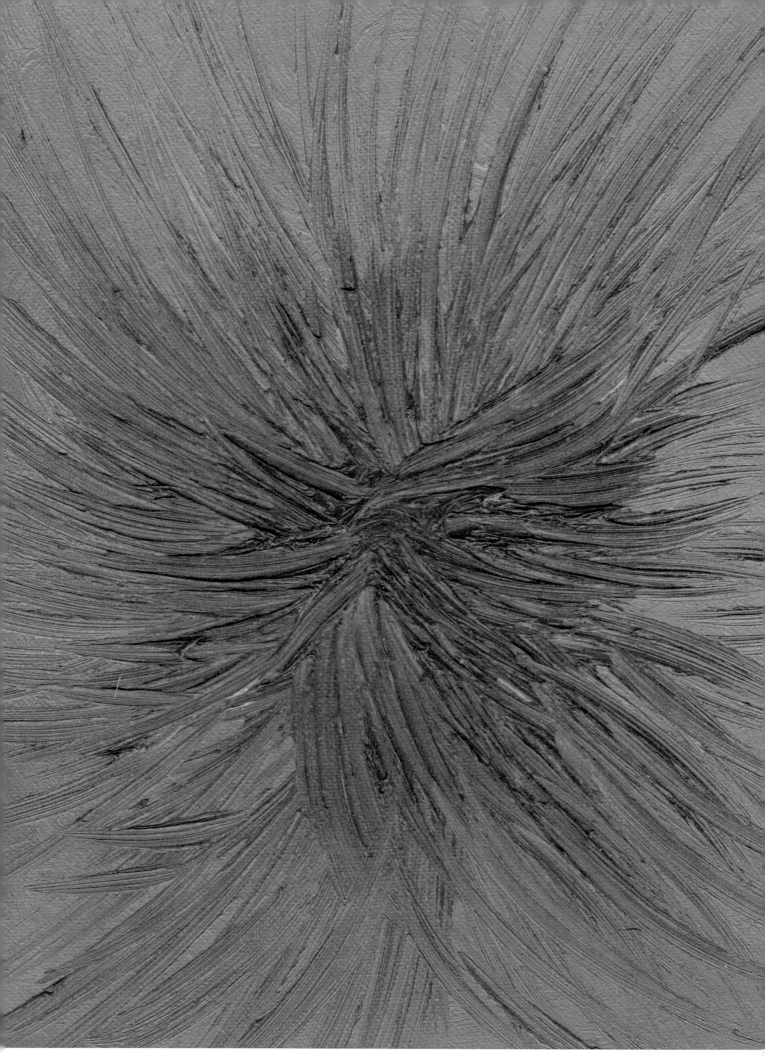

Printed in the United States
By Bookmasters